Bloody Shards in Trembling Hands

Victoria Valenzuela

Bloody Shards in Trembling Hands © 2022
Victoria Valenzuela

All rights reserved.

No part of this publication may be
reproduced, stored in a retrieval system, or
transmitted, in any form or by any means,
electronic, mechanical, photocopying,
recording or otherwise, without the prior
written permission of the presenters.

Victoria Valenzuela asserts the moral right
to be identified as author of this work.

Presentation by *BookLeaf Publishing*

Web: www.bookleafpub.com

E-mail: info@bookleafpub.com

ISBN: 9789357612821

First edition 2022

DEDICATION

This book is for my Elva, who has saved my life in more ways than she knows.

ACKNOWLEDGEMENT

I would like to thank everyone who has ever supported or encouraged my writing. I love you all!

PREFACE

This book, although short, may be a rough ride. I write to make sense of the events that have happened in my life, and bring about my truth in them. I hope that others may find their truths here too, and feel less alone in them.

Muse

I tell myself I will
    No longer write about you.
I will disallow you
    To be my muse.
I will refuse
    The inspiration you bring me.
I will leave alone
    The swelling of love you bring.
I will ignore
    The butterflies until they die of hunger.
I will pretend
    That you are not everything I want.
I will pretend
    That you are not my favorite person.
I will...
    Fail at it all...
        Again.

Still Lake

No, no honey, it's not you.
It's not you this time.
He says he loves you,
But is not in love with you.
Not for anything that you are,
Or that you are not.
But for his lack of love to fall in.

And though your heart weeps
And overflows with the love you drown in,
This is the love you accept.
Because-
At least there is honesty in his emotions.
For once it is not the dry river of you
Nor the broken dam of you
That results in a departure.

His still lake waters are tried and true.

Worthy

You give me droplets and
I can pretend that you give me an ocean.
I will fabricate these corals,
Those fish, and even a few sharks.

You give me a few grains of sand and
I create my own desert.
I manufacture dunes, cacti,
And maybe a small oasis.

You give me the smallest sapling and
I will imagine myself a rainforest.
Listen to those birds sing as the broad leaves,
Heavy with dew, surround me.

You exhale a whisper to me, and
I use your sweet nothings to fill my oxygen
tanks,
Send a gust across the land,
And fly a paper plane across the room.

You gift me a sliver of your soul,
and I cherish it so long as I live,
have you be a part of me.

We accept the love we think we deserve,
and I grow it until you are deserving of me.

Oasis

Skin to skin-
The most intimate of actions.
Rough hands to the
softest parts of my broken spine.
Cradle the excessive curvature-
which you love so.
Chipped nails get caught in hair
Tearing strand and strand.
Kiss these chapped lips.
Caress the damage.
Coddle the destruction.
Lay claim to this waste.

Your touch is an oasis in this desert called body.
A sweet refuge from the harsh surroundings.

You are nourishment.
Hydration.
Rest.

Oasis-
All you can be for me.
You cannot turn my arid desert
into a lush rainforest.

Amphibious

I sink as I wait for you.
Slowly feeling your love leave.
I wait quietly as the water rises.
I hold my breath.
Trusting your return.
My lungs burn the realization into me.
You have left me to drown.
Instinct kicks in.
The initial gulp of water.
Burns more than the lack of oxygen.
The second gulp reveals less ache.
Amphibious.
I will not die for lack of you.

Differences

You say you love me
The best way that you can.
I can only love you
With all that I have.
You say that you can only trust me
This much,
Hardly at all.
I can only trust you
With my heart on a platter.
You say our differences are
Far too distinct, alienating.
I say I love you just the same.
I long to understand
the way that you think.

Field Trip

My mind took me for a field trip.
It took a left turn into the woods.
These despairing woods
That are no strangers to my visits.

The trees of my memories are dying
One day I will not recognize these trees,
Every time I visit
They have changed.
Each time they twist and deform.

One day these will no longer be my trees.
They will fade out of my life and
My mind will take a left turn
Into empty fields.

Makeup

Maybe it's a trauma bond
Maybe it's Maybelline.
I use your love to cover up the pain.
Pretend it makes it go away
If you can't see it then it doesn't exist.
I never developed object permanence.
This foundation may mask the bruise,
But I never learned to color match.
The lipstick may cover up that split,
But I'll be damned if it doesn't create a lisp.

Guilt

I have never escaped the guilt.
It doesn't hang around like a low lying cloud.
This guilt is sticky.
Never quite able to get clean.
It's been five years since
You broke me apart.
And you couldn't ever care less.
But I carry the guilt in my backpack
With my wallet, keys, phone,
and your prison paperwork.
You always told me it was my fault.
And the guilt mimics your voice.

Dreams

They hide in the shadows of our minds.
You push them back and back.
The memories fade from your consciousness,
But at night, when we lay at rest, relax
They creep back in with a vengeance.
The fear that you stuffed in a box,
The terror shoved under the bed,
The nightmares feel real-
Steal you away from reality.

You wake with anxiety,
But you wake.
The past may haunt you,
But it can't hurt you.
You wake to your new life.
Full of hope, love, and goals to achieve.
Every waking day is a new victory.

Black Hole

When the events are so heavy
They weigh on your chest.
Not holding you in place like an anchor,
Pulling you down like a cartoon anvil.
One afer another
The chest collapses,
But the weight keeps coming.
You bury it, crushing it to make it fit.
Compound the trauma.
Compound the weight.
Those buried anvils explode.
Implode.
"How beautiful."
As the supernova blinds you
In the blink of an eye.
Inside it feels like eternity-
How beautiful is my destruction.
The event horizon cannot be escaped.
I pull you in,
dragging you until you disappear.

Step Up

Have you stepped up yet, Victoria?
Have you stepped into this role?
Is this all you ever wanted?
When you were young and naïve
And had no idea of what was to come?
Is this what you expected?
As you daydreamed about your future?

Have you stepped up yet, Victoria?
Stepped into everything you were shoved into?
All the decisions made for you?
When others decided your best interest?
When you actually thought all was well
And your love was tainted by those rose colored
glasses?

Have you stepped up yet, Victoria?
As things were piled higher on your plate?
Juggling all of your responsibilities
Like a klutzy clown or the worst debutant?
Trying to be everything to everyone
And being nothing to anyone
And somehow even less for yourself.

Temple

We are the temple
He came in,
Raped, ravaged and destroyed.
Tore down the altar and
Crushed our pillars
We stood devastated.
The task of fixing ourselves -
Impossible.
But brick by brick.
Moment by moment.
It comes up.
A new temple.
Different.
Beautiful.
Nothing like before.

Institution White

Institution white.
The sterile color of healing.
The color of the pain
Once the pills numb it out.
Like the healing and pain isn't mottled-
Browns, purples, and greens.

Institution white.
The strong straps on the table.
When they decide you're just a little too happy
And need to calm down.
Like they're wanting you to slice any feeling out.

Institution white.
The blinding color of the scrubs.
Bright like the blues and reds of poisonous
frogs.
Warning- Danger.

Institution white.
The blank paper the doctor took notes on
When they ask what exactly led you to this?
What makes you want to die?
Like they actually care about anything besides

Kicking your unstable ass out at the 30 minute mark.

Family Tree

We know what a family should look like.
The sprawling branches
In every direction.
The tree trunk strong-
Withstanding.
The roots firmly planted
Healthy.
But we have been cut off.
The tree wrongly pruned.
Disconnected from the ancestors.
Strangers to our tribe.
Sins of the father,
Shame of the mother.
Leave children in the dark
They must make their own home--
Set root in nourishing soil.

Mother Wound

The mother wound-
The mother who should not wound.
The mother who does nothing but wound.
The wound is not solitary,
It exists in our family trees.
Generational.
Passed down from unloved mother,
To unloved daughter.
Unloveable.
We are taught-
If we are not useful,
What is the use in loving us?

Keys

People always talk about
Keys opening doors for us.
The key to success, happiness,
Healing, love and life.
All you need are the right keys
To get everything you could ever want.

What say you of the keys
That lock the closet doors from the outside?
The creatures behind the sturdy wood
Scratch and bang,
But can never leave.
Stringing that key around your neck,
Just in case.

And what about the keys
That firmly lock doors behind us?
Hearing the metal clicking
Into place as the mechanisms shift.
Feeling the relief,
A weight off your chest,
a tornado from your mind.

As simple as tossing

An old key in the trash,
Destined to never return.
Leaving an old life behind.
Finally closure and distance.

Eat

Do you eat your feelings?
Like a whole bag of chips
Two bowls of popcorn
A hamburger
Super-size the fries and drink?
The salty savory sweet
Caressing your tongue
And dropping just past
That hole you long to fill?

Or do your feelings eat you?
Like the sweetest,
Saddest delicacy?
From the inside out,
Savoring every hope,
Dream and aspiration,
Along with your arteries,
Kidneys and stomach lining?

Roads

We build roads as links between people.
Our longing for connection making
The journey worth the risk.
Louis and Clark
Forging new trails, meeting and connecting
with new people.
Never knowing to what that may lead
Or where it may bring us.
Old roads, familiar tracks.
The roadside attractions-
Our inside jokes and shared memories
Along the way.
Oh, all those ghosts?
Products of the twists and turns
Our lives have taken.
Our Route 66,
Well traveled and well loved.
Our common path.
Falling into disrepair-
cracked asphalt and potholes
As we fail to maintain
And repair our relationships.
The quick builds,
Too quick, too new, too cheap?
Unsupported foundation

Do not hold up against the traffic.

Rain

24

The sweet tranquility of the world
After a good rain.
The smell of cleansing and renewal.
After the dust of the day has settled.
Late at night,
Partially hidden moon.
Just bright enough.
The sounds of the world are muffled.
Maybe just for those of us who sit and hope
Longing for the rainy days.
The soft rain in a world that's just too loud.

Time

I feel the hours melt away.
I hear the seconds tick on by.
I live for nights like this-
Borrowing anothers life.
I watch others existances pass
Through my mind.
Watch their rage and passion,
I drown my pain in theirs.
As I watch the sky light up,
As the night becomes day,
I return to myself.
The mediocre life I long to escape.

www.ingramcontent.com/pod-product-compliance
Lightning Source LLC
Chambersburg PA
CBHW070723160726
48003CB00006BA/2350